MAKEUP FACE CHARTS

NAME : ___________________________

PHONE : ___________________________

EMAIL : ___________________________

TABLE OF CONTENTS

CLIENT'S INFORMATION	PAGE NUMBER

TABLE OF CONTENTS

CLIENT'S INFORMATION	PAGE NUMBER

FACE CHART

MAKE UP LOOK

Daytime ☐ Evening ☐ Wedding ☐ Party ☐ Other ☐

Client Name : _____________________ Date : _____________

Adresse : _____________________

phone : _____________________

Skin	
Eyes	
Lips	
Face	

Feedback / Notes :

____

____

____

1

FACE CHART

MAKE UP LOOK

Daytime ☐ Evening ☐ Wedding ☐ Party ☐ Other ☐

Client Name : ________________________   Date : ________

Adresse : ________________________

phone : ________________________

Skin	
Eyes	
Lips	
Face	

Feedback / Notes :

FACE CHART

MAKE UP LOOK

Daytime ☐ Evening ☐ Wedding ☐ Party ☐ Other ☐

Client Name : ______________________ Date : __________

Adresse : ______________________

phone : ______________________

Skin	____________________________
Eyes	____________________________
Lips	____________________________
Face	____________________________

Feedback / Notes :

____

____

____

FACE CHART

MAKE UP LOOK

Daytime ☐ Evening ☐ Wedding ☐ Party ☐ Other ☐

Client Name : _______________   Date : _______________

Adresse   : _______________

phone   : _______________

Skin	
Eyes	
Lips	
Face	

Feedback / Notes :

MAKE UP LOOK

Daytime ☐ Evening ☐ Wedding ☐ Party ☐ Other ☐

Client Name : ________________________ Date : ________________

Adresse : ________________________

phone : ________________________

Skin	________________________
Eyes	________________________
Lips	________________________
Face	________________________

Feedback / Notes :

____

____

____

FACE CHART

MAKE UP LOOK

Daytime ☐ Evening ☐ Wedding ☐ Party ☐ Other ☐

Client Name : ________________________ Date : ____________

Adresse : ________________________

phone : ________________________

Skin	
Eyes	
Lips	
Face	

Feedback / Notes :

MAKE UP LOOK

Daytime ☐ Evening ☐ Wedding ☐ Party ☐ Other ☐

Client Name : _______________________ Date : _________

 Adresse : _______________________

phone : _______________________

Skin	_______________________ _______________________
Eyes	_______________________ _______________________
Lips	_______________________ _______________________
Face	_______________________ _______________________

Feedback / Notes :

____

____

____

FACE CHART

MAKE UP LOOK

Daytime ☐ Evening ☐ Wedding ☐ Party ☐ Other ☐

Client Name : _______________________ Date : __________

Adresse : _______________________

phone : _______________________

Skin	
Eyes	
Lips	
Face	

Feedback / Notes :

____

____

____

FACE CHART

MAKE UP LOOK

Daytime ☐ Evening ☐ Wedding ☐ Party ☐ Other ☐

Client Name : _______________________ Date : _____________

Adresse : _____________________________

phone : _____________________________

Skin	__________________________ __________________________
Eyes	__________________________ __________________________
Lips	__________________________ __________________________
Face	__________________________ __________________________

Feedback / Notes :

____

____

____

MAKE UP LOOK

Daytime ☐ Evening ☐ Wedding ☐ Party ☐ Other ☐

Client Name : _______________________   Date : _______________

Adresse   : _______________________

phone   : _______________________

Skin	
Eyes	
Lips	
Face	

Feedback / Notes :

____

____

____

MAKE UP LOOK

Daytime ☐ Evening ☐ Wedding ☐ Party ☐ Other ☐

Client Name : ________________________ Date : ____________

Adresse : ________________________

phone : ________________________

Skin	
Eyes	
Lips	
Face	

Feedback / Notes :

____

____

____

FACE CHART

MAKE UP LOOK

Daytime ☐ Evening ☐ Wedding ☐ Party ☐ Other ☐

Client Name : _________________________   Date : _________

Adresse   : _________________________

phone   : _________________________

Skin	
Eyes	
Lips	
Face	

Feedback / Notes :

____

____

____

FACE CHART

MAKE UP LOOK

Daytime ☐ Evening ☐ Wedding ☐ Party ☐ Other ☐

Client Name : _____________________ Date : _____________

Adresse : _____________________

phone : _____________________

Skin	_____________________
Eyes	_____________________
Lips	_____________________
Face	_____________________

Feedback / Notes :

____

FACE CHART

MAKE UP LOOK

Daytime ☐ Evening ☐ Wedding ☐ Party ☐ Other ☐

Client Name : _________________________   Date : _________

Adresse : _________________________

phone : _________________________

Skin	
Eyes	
Lips	
Face	

Feedback / Notes :

FACE CHART

MAKE UP LOOK

Daytime ☐ Evening ☐ Wedding ☐ Party ☐ Other ☐

Client Name : _________________________ Date : _____________

Adresse : _________________________

phone : _________________________

Skin	
Eyes	
Lips	
Face	

Feedback / Notes :

____

____

____

16

FACE CHART

MAKE UP LOOK

Daytime ☐ Evening ☐ Wedding ☐ Party ☐ Other ☐

Client Name   : _________________________   Date   : _________

Adresse   : _________________________

phone   : _________________________

Skin	
Eyes	
Lips	
Face	

Feedback / Notes :

____

____

____

FACE CHART

MAKE UP LOOK

Daytime ☐ Evening ☐ Wedding ☐ Party ☐ Other ☐

Client Name : ______________________   Date : ___________

Adresse : ______________________

phone : ______________________

Skin	
Eyes	
Lips	
Face	

Feedback / Notes :

____

____

____

FACE CHART

MAKE UP LOOK

Daytime ☐ Evening ☐ Wedding ☐ Party ☐ Other ☐

Client Name : _____________________   Date : _____________

Adresse : _____________________

phone : _____________________

Skin	_____________________
Eyes	_____________________
Lips	_____________________
Face	_____________________

Feedback / Notes :

____

FACE CHART

MAKE UP LOOK

Daytime ☐ Evening ☐ Wedding ☐ Party ☐ Other ☐

Client Name : _______________   Date : _______________

Adresse : _______________

phone : _______________

Skin	
Eyes	
Lips	
Face	

Feedback / Notes :

FACE CHART

MAKE UP LOOK

Daytime ☐ Evening ☐ Wedding ☐ Party ☐ Other ☐

Client Name : ___________________________ Date : ___________

Adresse : ___________________________

phone : ___________________________

Skin	
Eyes	
Lips	
Face	

Feedback / Notes :

____

____

____

FACE CHART

MAKE UP LOOK

Daytime ☐ Evening ☐ Wedding ☐ Party ☐ Other ☐

Client Name : _____________ Date : _____________

Adresse : _____________

phone : _____________

Skin	
Eyes	
Lips	
Face	

Feedback / Notes :

MAKE UP LOOK

Daytime ☐ Evening ☐ Wedding ☐ Party ☐ Other ☐

Client Name : _______________________ Date : _______________

Adresse : _______________________

phone : _______________________

Skin	
Eyes	
Lips	
Face	

Feedback / Notes :

____

____

____

FACE CHART

MAKE UP LOOK

Daytime ☐ Evening ☐ Wedding ☐ Party ☐ Other ☐

Client Name : ______________________   Date : ______________

Adresse   : ______________________

phone   : ______________________

Skin	________________________ ________________________
Eyes	________________________ ________________________
Lips	________________________ ________________________
Face	________________________ ________________________

Feedback / Notes :

____

____

____

24

FACE CHART

MAKE UP LOOK

Daytime ☐ Evening ☐ Wedding ☐ Party ☐ Other ☐

Client Name : _______________________ Date : _______________

Adresse : _______________________________

phone : _______________________________

Skin	
Eyes	
Lips	
Face	

Feedback / Notes :

____

____

____

25

FACE CHART

MAKE UP LOOK

Daytime ☐ Evening ☐ Wedding ☐ Party ☐ Other ☐

Client Name : ___________________ Date : ___________

Adresse : ___________________

phone : ___________________

Skin	
Eyes	
Lips	
Face	

Feedback / Notes :

____

____

____

FACE CHART

MAKE UP LOOK

Daytime ☐ Evening ☐ Wedding ☐ Party ☐ Other ☐

Client Name : _______________________ Date : _____________

Adresse : _______________________

phone : _______________________

Skin	
Eyes	
Lips	
Face	

Feedback / Notes :

FACE CHART

MAKE UP LOOK

Daytime ☐ Evening ☐ Wedding ☐ Party ☐ Other ☐

Client Name : _______________________ Date : _______________

Adresse : _______________________

phone : _______________________

Skin	
Eyes	
Lips	
Face	

Feedback / Notes :

____

____

____

FACE CHART

MAKE UP LOOK

Daytime ☐ Evening ☐ Wedding ☐ Party ☐ Other ☐

Client Name : ________________________   Date : __________

Adresse   : ________________________

phone   : ________________________

Skin	____________________
Eyes	____________________
Lips	____________________
Face	____________________

Feedback / Notes :

____

____

____

FACE CHART

MAKE UP LOOK

Daytime ☐ Evening ☐ Wedding ☐ Party ☐ Other ☐

Client Name : __________________________   Date : __________

Adresse   : __________________________

phone   : __________________________

Skin	
Eyes	
Lips	
Face	

Feedback / Notes :

____

____

____

FACE CHART

MAKE UP LOOK

Daytime ☐ Evening ☐ Wedding ☐ Party ☐ Other ☐

Client Name : ______________________ Date : ______________

Adresse : ______________________

phone : ______________________

Skin	
Eyes	
Lips	
Face	

Feedback / Notes :

FACE CHART

MAKE UP LOOK

Daytime ☐ Evening ☐ Wedding ☐ Party ☐ Other ☐

Client Name : ________________________ Date : ____________

Adresse : ________________________

phone : ________________________

Skin	
Eyes	
Lips	
Face	

Feedback / Notes :

____

____

____

FACE CHART

MAKE UP LOOK

Daytime ☐ Evening ☐ Wedding ☐ Party ☐ Other ☐

Client Name : _____________________ Date : __________

Adresse : _____________________

phone : _____________________

Skin	
Eyes	
Lips	
Face	

Feedback / Notes :

____

____

____

FACE CHART

MAKE UP LOOK

Daytime ☐ Evening ☐ Wedding ☐ Party ☐ Other ☐

Client Name : _______________________   Date : _______________

Adresse   : _______________________

phone   : _______________________

Skin	_______________________
Eyes	_______________________
Lips	_______________________
Face	_______________________

Feedback / Notes :

____

____

____

FACE CHART

MAKE UP LOOK

Daytime ☐ Evening ☐ Wedding ☐ Party ☐ Other ☐

Client Name : _______________________ Date : _______________

Adresse : _______________________

phone : _______________________

Skin	__________________________
Eyes	__________________________
Lips	__________________________
Face	__________________________

Feedback / Notes :

____

____

____

FACE CHART

MAKE UP LOOK

Daytime ☐ Evening ☐ Wedding ☐ Party ☐ Other ☐

Client Name : _______________________ Date : _______

Adresse   : _______________________

phone   : _______________________

Skin	___________________________ ___________________________
Eyes	___________________________ ___________________________
Lips	___________________________ ___________________________
Face	___________________________ ___________________________

Feedback / Notes :

____

____

____

FACE CHART

MAKE UP LOOK

Daytime ☐ Evening ☐ Wedding ☐ Party ☐ Other ☐

Client Name : _______________   Date : _______________

Adresse : _______________

phone : _______________

Skin	
Eyes	
Lips	
Face	

Feedback / Notes :

MAKE UP LOOK

Daytime ☐ Evening ☐ Wedding ☐ Party ☐ Other ☐

Client Name : ___________________   Date : ___________

Adresse   : ___________________

phone   : ___________________

Skin	__________________________ __________________________
Eyes	__________________________ __________________________
Lips	__________________________ __________________________
Face	__________________________ __________________________

Feedback / Notes :

____

____

____

FACE CHART

MAKE UP LOOK

Daytime ☐ Evening ☐ Wedding ☐ Party ☐ Other ☐

Client Name : _______________________   Date : _______________

Adresse   : _______________________

phone   : _______________________

Skin	
Eyes	
Lips	
Face	

Feedback / Notes :

____

____

____

FACE CHART

MAKE UP LOOK

Daytime ☐ Evening ☐ Wedding ☐ Party ☐ Other ☐

Client Name : _____________________ Date : _____________

Adresse : _____________________

phone : _____________________

Skin	
Eyes	
Lips	
Face	

Feedback / Notes :

FACE CHART

MAKE UP LOOK

Daytime ☐ Evening ☐ Wedding ☐ Party ☐ Other ☐

Client Name : _______________   Date : _______________

Adresse   : _______________

phone   : _______________

Skin	
Eyes	
Lips	
Face	

Feedback / Notes :

____

____

____